Shaquille

Revised Edition

O'Neal

By Ross Bernstein

AMAZING
ATHLETES

Lerner Publications Comp

D1378170

Lerner Publications Company
A division of Lerner Publishing Group, Inc.
241 First Avenue North
Minneapolis, MN 55401 U.S.A.

Website address: www.lernerbooks.com

Library of Congress Cataloging-in-Publication Data

Bernstein, Ross.
    Shaquille O'Neal / by Ross Bernstein.
      p.   cm. — (Amazing athletes)
    Includes bibliographical references and index.
    ISBN 978-0-7613-4488-9 (lib. bdg. : alk. paper)
    1. O'Neal, Shaquille—Juvenile literature. 2. Basketball players—United States—Biography—
Juvenile literature. I. Title.
    GV884.O54B47 2009
    796.323'092—dc22 [B]   2008028270

Manufactured in the United States of America
1 2 3 4 5 6 – BP – 14 13 12 11 10 09

TABLE OF CONTENTS

The San Antonio Spurs couldn't stop Shaq near the basket.

ONE OF THE BEST

Shaquille O'Neal crouched near the basket. Up the court, teammate Grant Hill held the ball. He passed to Shaq. Shaq caught the ball between his big hands. He spun around a **defender** and leaped into the air to take a six-foot **jump shot**. Swish! Two points!

Shaq and his team, the Phoenix Suns, were playing against the San Antonio Spurs during the 2007–2008 **regular season**. This was an important game for Shaq and the Suns. The Spurs and the Suns had been **rivals** for a long time. Both teams were trying to make it to the **playoffs**. Shaq also had another reason to play hard. He had turned 36-years-old three days earlier. He wanted to prove to himself that he still had what it takes to play with the pros.

Shaq is bigger than most pro basketball players.

Shaq jumps for a slam dunk.

Shaq was playing hard. He jumped high into the air to make basket after basket. Shaq even jumped into the stands to catch a loose ball! When he saw the ball fly past him, he ran towards the edge of the court to catch it. He grabbed the ball and threw it back to one of his teammates. But he couldn't slow down. Shaq leaped over the first two rows of seats and landed in the third row! Shaq was earning his nickname: "Superman."

The game was close. But Shaq and the Suns kept the pressure on. With only two and a half minutes left in the game, the two teams were tied at 85 points. Then the Suns took the lead. When the game ended, the Suns had won, 94–87.

Shaq had scored 14 points, grabbed 16 **rebounds**, and swatted two **blocked shots**. His two blocks pushed him up to 2,500 blocked shots in his career. Shaq became just the third player in National Basketball Association (NBA) history to reach 26,000 points, 11,500 rebounds, and 2,500 blocked shots in his career. After 16 seasons in the NBA, Shaq was still setting records!

The record-setting **center** is happy to play in Phoenix. "I love playing for [former Suns' coach Mike D'Antoni]," Shaq said, "and I love playing with these guys."

Former Suns' coach Mike D'Antoni was glad to have Shaq on the team.

Philip and Lucille Harrison stand behind their children *(left to right)*: Lateefah, Ayesha, Jamal, and Shaquille.

BOUNCING AROUND

Shaquille Rashaun O'Neal was born in Newark, New Jersey, on March 6, 1972. Shaq's mother's name is Lucille O'Neal. Shaq's stepfather's name is Philip Harrison. Harrison was a sergeant in the U.S. Army. He was very strict. He wanted his children to work hard in school and stay out of trouble. Philip Harrison was tough on Shaq, but Shaq loves and respects him.

Shaq's family moved around to many different army bases. When Shaq was a kid, his family moved from New Jersey to Georgia to Germany and finally to Texas. Shaq always had to make new friends. But he got to know people by telling jokes and making his classmates laugh.

Shaq was always the biggest kid in his class. By the time he was 13, he was a whopping six feet eight inches tall. He wore size 17 shoes!

Shaq loved to play sports. Basketball was his favorite game, and he played it whenever he could. One summer, Shaq attended a **basketball camp.** A coach named Dale Brown ran the camp. Coach Brown was the head basketball coach at Louisiana State University (LSU) in Baton Rouge, Louisiana.

Shaq's childhood hero was Philadelphia 76ers superstar Julius "Dr. J" Erving. Dr. J was known for his high-flying dunks, and Shaq wanted to be just like him.

Coach Brown quickly saw that Shaq had the chance to be a great player. Not only was Shaq tall, he was also very strong. But he was only 14 and kind of clumsy. Coach Brown worked with Shaq and told him to practice as much as he could. Coach Brown told Shaq that if he worked hard, he could be a great player. So Shaq practiced with his friends, with his dad, and by himself. He even slept with his basketball each night. Shaq dreamed of playing in the NBA.

LSU coach Dale Brown saw that Shaq had promise as a basketball player and as a person.

Shaq could dunk on kids even in high school.

UNSTOPPABLE

When Shaq was in high school, he and his family moved to San Antonio, Texas. By then, he was six feet eleven inches tall! Shaq joined his high school team and soon became its star player. All of his hard work and practice was payin off. Shaq was unstoppable.

In high school, Shaq was so big that other teams didn't want to play against him. Said one coach, "We were beat as soon as our players got a look at Shaquille."

Shaq was head and shoulders above the other kids on the court.

He was so big and strong, no one could keep him from scoring or grabbing rebounds. During his junior and senior years, Shaq averaged 32 points, 22 rebounds, and 8 blocked shots per game. He led his team to a 68–1 record and a state championship.

Basketball experts were calling Shaq the best high school player in the country. Nearly every college in the United States wanted him on its team. But Shaq decided to play for his old friend Coach Brown at LSU.

Shaq started college during the fall of 1989. At first, he struggled. The college game was faster, and the players were much better.

Shaq played hard for the fans at LSU.

After just three seasons of college basketball, Shaq was ready to move on to the NBA.

But Shaq hung tough. He went to class and studied hard. And he practiced whenever he could. Shaq's passing, shooting, and scoring all improved. In his last two seasons at LSU, Shaq averaged nearly 22 points, 14 rebounds, and 5 blocked shots per game. Basketball experts voted him College Basketball Player of the Year.

As the best college player, Shaq decided to enter the **NBA draft.** His NBA dream was about to come true! That year, the Orlando Magic had the number one overall pick. The Magic chose the very best—Shaquille O'Neal.

Coach Brown admired Shaq's hard work. "I've never coached a player who's improved so much from one year to the next," he said.

Shaq was all smiles after being drafted number one by the Orlando Magic.

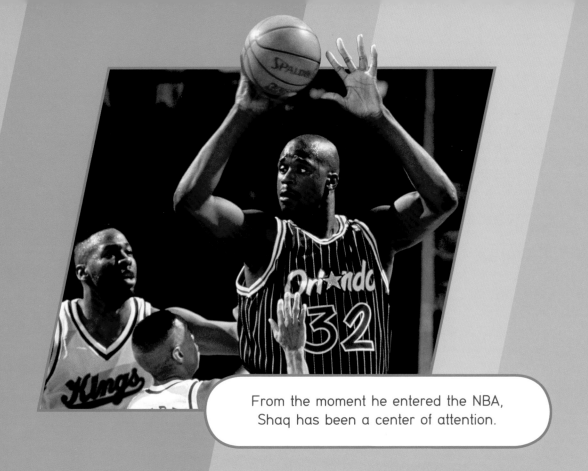

From the moment he entered the NBA, Shaq has been a center of attention.

A DREAM COME TRUE

Shaq signed a **contract** with the Magic for $41 million! He bought a mansion in Orlando, Florida, and several fancy cars. He appeared on billboards, magazine covers, TV commercials, and TV talk shows.

Just like that, Shaq was rich and famous. But money and fame weren't the most important things to him. He wanted to win an NBA championship. And he wanted to be the best basketball player he could be.

During his **rookie** season, Shaq took the NBA by storm. Tens of thousands of fans showed up at games to watch him play.

Shaq has appeared in many TV commercials. Here he is filming an ad for Pepsi.

Millions more watched Orlando Magic games on TV. Shaq made sure to give everyone a good show. He averaged 23 points and 14 rebounds a game. Shaq was named NBA Rookie of the Year.

In Shaq's second season, the Magic won 50 games and made the playoffs for the first time. Yet the Indiana Pacers beat the Magic in the first round of the playoffs.

Shaq and the Magic had a super 1994–1995 season. They won 57 games. Shaq led the league

In his rookie season, Shaq made a whopping 322 dunks—out of a total of 743 baskets.

in scoring, averaging 29 points per game. In the playoffs, the Magic made it all the way to the 1995 NBA Finals.

All of a sudden, Shaq was four wins away from being a champion! But the Houston Rockets swept the Magic in four games. Shaq was angry and disappointed. He promised to do better next year.

But the Magic had missed their chance. The next season, Michael Jordan and the mighty Chicago Bulls were the league's best team. In the playoffs, the Bulls beat up on the Magic. Once again, Shaq's season ended in defeat.

"I'm happy the fans like to see me play," says Shaq. "I'm 7-foot-1, 300 pounds. I can dunk hard. I slide on the floor. I get rebounds. People like to see that. If I was a fan, I'd want to see Shaq play, too."

In the summer of 1996, Shaq was selected to play for the U.S. Olympic Basketball Team in Atlanta. Nicknamed the Dream Team, the group of NBA superstars won the gold medal.

Shaq was frustrated. He was tired of losing in the playoffs. He wanted to make a change. His contract had expired, and he was a **free agent.** This meant he could sign with any team that wanted him. And every team in the league wanted Shaq!

Shaq made a big impact with the Los Angeles Lakers.

LOOKING AHEAD

Shaq decided to sign with the Los Angeles Lakers in 1996. Shaq and the Lakers had a hard time winning at first. Shaq missed lots of games because of injuries. Even when the Lakers made it to the playoffs, they didn't get very far.

Shaq was the strongest player on the court during the 2000 NBA Finals.

The Lakers hit their stride during the 1999–2000 season. Shaq won the **NBA Most Valuable Player Award**, and the Lakers rolled to the **NBA Finals**. In Game Six of the Finals, Shaq scored 41 points to help the Lakers beat the Indiana Pacers 116–111. The Lakers had won the championship! Shaq was named Most Valuable Player (MVP) of the series.

Shaq and the Lakers were unstoppable. They stormed to two more championships in 2000–2001 and 2001–2002. Shaq was named MVP of the series both years.

By now Shaq was looking for a new challenge. In 2004 he was traded to the Miami Heat. He led his new team to victory in the NBA Finals in 2005–2006. Shaq had been in the NBA for fourteen years and won four championships. But he wasn't finished yet. He knew he could win even more NBA titles.

Shaq led the Miami Heat to victory in the 2006 NBA Finals.

In 2008, Shaq asked to be traded. The Heat were having trouble winning games. Shaq wasn't having fun in Miami. He knew he could play better on a new team. He joined the Phoenix Suns during the 2007–2008 season and moved to Arizona.

Shaq was happy to get a new start with a new team.

Shaq talks with new teammates Gordan Giricek (*left*) and Leandro Barbosa (*right*).

Shaq is excited to play for the Suns. "I'm having a great time," he says. "I'm in the best shape of my life. I'm with a good organization."

Even though Shaq is having fun, he knows he won't be in the NBA forever. At age 36, he is getting ready to retire from pro basketball. After so many years of dominating the court, Shaq is just happy to still be playing the game he loves.

For Shaq, retiring doesn't mean slowing down. He has many interests outside of basketball. He has starred in films and recorded rap albums. He has volunteered with police departments in Los Angeles, Miami, and Phoenix. He talks to kids about staying safe on the Internet. In 2007, he hosted a television

show to teach kids how to stay in shape. Shaq has six children of his own. Keeping kids safe and healthy is very important to him.

Shaq is interested in working as a police officer.

Shaq even has his own company! Boraie-O'Neal Urban Development Partnership invests money in building homes and other buildings that will improve cities. One of its projects is a new apartment building in Newark, New Jersey, where Shaq was born. Shaq is happy to find a way to help his hometown. "I've always believed that no success is complete without giving back to the place you call home," he said.

Shaq is active in his community. In 2008, he helped give food to poor families in Arizona.

Shaq still loves to play basketball.

Shaq's career as a basketball legend is nearing its end. But by staying active as an actor, role model, and businessman, Shaq's success is far from complete.

Selected Career Highlights

2007–2008   Became third player in NBA history to score 26,000 points, grab 11,500 rebounds, and block 2,500 shots

2006–2007   Averaged 17.3 points per game

2005–2006   Selected for Eastern Conference All-Stars

2004–2005   Named to All-NBA First Team
Named the *Sporting News* Player of the Year
Selected for Eastern Conference All-Stars

2005–2006   Named to 2006 NBA All-StarTeam

2004–2005   Named to 2005 NBA All-StarTeam
Grabbed 10,000th career rebound at a game in Utah

2003–2004   Voted most valuable player of 2004 NBA All-Star Game

2002–2003   Named to 2003 NBA All-Star Team

2001–2002   Named to All-NBA First Team
Named most valuable player of NBA Finals

2000–2001   Named most valuable player of NBA Finals
Named to All-NBA First Team

1999–2000   Voted NBA's most valuable player
Named to All-NBA First Team
Named most valuable player of NBA Finals
Led NBA in scoring with 29.7 points per game
Named co-MVP of All-star game

1997–1998   Named to All-NBA First Team

1996–1997   Named as one of the 50 greatest players in NBA history

1995–1996   Won gold medal as member of U.S. Olympic Basketball Team at 1996 Olympic Games in Atlanta

1994–1995   Led the NBA in scoring with 29.3 points per game

1993–1994   Won gold medal with U.S. basketball team at the World Championships in Toronto, Canada

1992–1993   Named NBA Rookie of the Year

Glossary

basketball camp: a camp where kids go to learn about playing basketball

blocked shots: when players stop other players' shot attempts by striking the ball

center: a player on a basketball team who usually plays close to the basket

contract: a written agreement between a player and a team. A contract usually says how much the player will be paid and how long he or she will play for the team.

defender: a player who tries to stop his opponent from scoring

free agent: a player who is free to sign with any team

jump shot: a shot in which a player shoots the ball into the basket while leaping high into the air

NBA draft: a yearly event in which NBA teams select players to play for them. The teams with the worst records get the top picks in the draft.

NBA Finals: the NBA's championship series. The team that wins four games in the series becomes the NBA champion.

NBA Most Valuable Player Award: an award given out each year to the most valuable player in the league

playoffs: the postseason tournament held to decide who is the NBA champion. The NBA playoffs have four rounds, and a team must win four games in each round to win the championship.

rebounds: balls grabbed after missed shots

regular season: the main part of a basketball season. The best teams go to the playoffs.

rivals: two teams fighting for what only one can have

rookie: a first-year player

Further Reading & Websites

Filbin, Dan. *Arizona*. Minneapolis: Lerner Publications Company, 2002.

Robinson, Tom. *Basketball Skills: How to Play Like a Pro*. Berkeley Heights, NJ: Enslow Publishers, Inc., 2008.

Ross, Jesse. *All-Star Sports Puzzles: Basketball*. Vancouver, Canada: Raincoast Books, 2007.

Savage, Jeff. *Steve Nash*. Minneapolis: Lerner Publications Company, 2007.

Phoenix Suns Website
http://www.nba.com/suns/
The official website of the Suns includes schedules, player news, player profiles, team history, and more.

Official NBA Website
http://www.nba.com
The official site of the National Basketball Association (NBA) includes news, notes, statistics, schedules, biographies, and general information.

Sports Illustrated Kids
http://www.sikids.com
The *Sports Illustrated Kids* website covers all sports, including basketball.

Index

Photo Acknowledgments

Photographs are used with the permission of: © Barry Gossage/NBAE/
Getty Images, pp. 4, 6, 7, 25, 27; © Garrett Ellwood/NBAE/Getty Images,
p. 5; © Andy King, p. 8; LSU Sports Information, p. 10; © Lynne Dobson,
Austin American Statesman, pp. 11, 12; © SportsChrome East/West/DLJ,
pp. 13, 14; © SportsChrome East/West/Brian Drake, pp. 15, 16; Courtesy of
Pepsico, Inc., p. 17; © SportsChrome East/West/Vincent Manniello, p. 18;
© SportsChrome East/West/Michael Zito, p. 21; © John W. McDonough/
SI/Icon SMI, p. 22; © Ronald Martinez/Getty Images, p. 23; © Nathaniel S.
Butler/NBAE/Getty Images, p. 24; © Mark Sullivan/WireImage/Getty Images,
p. 26; © Brian Babineau/NBAE/Getty Images, p. 28; © Ronald Martinez/Getty
Images, p. 29.

Cover: © Barry Gossage/Getty Images